It's Just...
WORK STUFF!

Concept by Matthew Richman
Written and illustrated by Stewart Williams

Email: Stewwriter@outlook.com
 Stewart Williams - Author/Illustrator
 stewart_williams_author

Text © 2023 by Stewart Williams
Illustrations copyright © 2023 by Stewart Williams
All rights reserved. No part of this book may be reproduced or transmitted in any form or by any means, electronic or mechanical, including photocopying, recording, or by any information storage or retrieval system without written permission of Stewart Williams.

For parents.

This book has been created for parents working in front-line emergency service roles who may be experiencing work stress including critical incident stress and PTSD.

It is intended to be used as a tool to stimulate family discussions and to help children better understand the changes they have seen in their mum or dad. In the absence of an explanation, children will often blame themselves for a changing home environment. This book aims to demystify PTSD and like illnesses and ensure children understand that it's not their fault and they are loved without exception.

This book has become a reality thanks to The Director of the Tasmanian Department of Police, Fire and Emergency Management Wellbeing Support Team, Matt Richman who approached me with the initial concept.

I would also like to acknowledge the enitre Wellbeing Support team for their input towards this book and for their unwavering, ongoing support to those that are struggling.

GET HELP NOW – 24 HOURS 6173 2873
wellbeing@dpfem.tas.gov.au

Special thanks also goes to:
Lisa Padden
Lisa Russel and her Catholic Care colleagues
My wife, Jane and kids, Ella and Lucy for their honest advice and in allowing me to spend so much time on this when it should have been with them.

And finally – thanks to an amazing Tasmanian company – **pro**create – who created the incredible platform which allowed me to design every element of this book in the one amazing app.

My dad is a police officer.

His job is really important.
It is all about keeping us safe.

My mum is a firefighter.

His job is to help people that are hurt or sick or lost.
It's a very important job.

I tried to be quieter, funnier and more helpful.
One day, I even did the dishes...
but nothing worked.

Dad said he never realised how much all these topsy turvy feelings upset our family, but now he understands that when he is sad, angry or scared... so are we.

Mum said that she won't get better straight away.
Just like if she had a broken leg.
So we just need to be patient and understanding...
and that can be hard sometimes.

Then she made me promise that if I ever feel scared, for me or anyone else, and I don't think I can speak to her or Dad, I will find another trusted adult to speak to.
Like Nan or my teacher!

Nan!

Dad is getting lots of help to get better, and he also said that all my love helps him too. So I know something I can do to help. I can tell him that I love him.
Every day.

So when mums or dads get tired, snappy or sad,
we need to try to remember...
it's not our fault!
It's not your fault.

Unless, of course, it's one of those times...

www.ingramcontent.com/pod-product-compliance
Lightning Source LLC
Chambersburg PA
CBHW041203290426
44109CB00003B/112